Zola Gets Hearing Aids

Copyright © 2020 ZOLA GETS HEARING AIDS, Narita Snead

Published by:
B.O.Y. Enterprises, Inc. on behalf of Narita Snead

Please direct all copyright inquiries to:
sneadnarita@gmail.com

No part of this book may be reproduced or transmitted in any form or by any means, electronic or mechanical, including photocopying and recording, or by any information storage or retrieval system, except as expressly permitted in writing by the copyright owner.

Illustrated by: Dawn Campbell

Interior Design - B.O.Y. Enterprises, Inc.

ISBN: 978-1-7350703-1-5

Printed in the United States of America.

ZOLA GETS HEARING AIDS

by Narita Snead

Illustrated by Dawn Campbell

Chapter 1

Zola hated going to the doctor. She hated it more than doing math homework or eating brussels sprouts.

This morning her mom had awakened her to go to a doctor's appointment. Zola lay in bed thinking about all the things that happened last week leading up to her doctor's appointment today.

Last week at school, Mrs. Smith asked Zola to go to the board and do a math problem. Zola was certain that she had written the problem and the answer correctly, but when she went back to her seat, she noticed that Mrs. Smith had the funniest expression on her face.

Zola did not pay it much attention and she simply continued to do schoolwork from her desk and wait for the bell to ring. Today was craft day at her after-school program and she was so excited to be making leather key chains. She decided she would make one for Daddy.

"He sure has a lot of keys. He would like my key chain."

The next morning while she was working hard on her spelling words, a voice rang out over the school intercom. "Mrs. Smith, please send Zola to the office."

"Zola, please put your things away and go to the principal's office."

Now what? I have not done a thing and they are calling me to the office, Zola thought to herself. She did as she was told, put her things away and got ready to walk down to the principal's office.

"Zola, Mrs. Adams will watch the class. I will walk with you to the office."

Oh boy, thought Zola, I must be in big trouble now. To Zola's surprise when she and Mrs. Smith got to the office, Mommy, Daddy, and Mrs. Gene were all sitting around a big table. Seeing all of these grown-ups could only mean one thing.

"I must be in trouble. Mommy and Daddy are going to be so mad at me."

Fearful of why everyone was meeting in the office, Zola began to cry.

"Don't cry, Zola," said Mommy.

"But Mommy everyone is here, so I must be in BIG trouble," said Zola.

"No, Zola. You are not in trouble," said Mrs. Gene.

"Zola, come over here and sit with Daddy," said Daddy.

Rubbing her eyes, Zola went over to her daddy and sat with him. Daddy was a big man with an even bigger voice. Zola suddenly did not feel scared with her daddy's arms wrapped around her.

"Zola?" Mrs. Smith called to her.

"Yes ma'am?" Zola said in a very small voice from her safe place in her daddy's arms.

"Zola, do you remember doing the math problem yesterday on the chalk board?"

"Yes, ma'am, but I got the answer right, didn't I?"

"Yes, Zola you did get the answer right, but when you turned your back to me, I spoke to you and called your name over 5 times and you did not hear me at all. We are all here today because we are concerned that you are not able to hear very well."

"Yes," Mrs. Gene chimed in. "Your mommy and daddy are going to take you to a special doctor to test your hearing."

"Ok," said Zola. What a relief she thought, at least I am not in trouble.

"Zola?"

"Yes, Mommy?"

"You are going to be just fine. Your Daddy and I are going to be there every step of the way and we love you no matter what."

Chapter 2

Zola sat up on the side of the bed. "I may as well get dressed and go to this new doctor. I don't know why everyone is so upset," she scowled. "Okay, I did not hear her calling me from the board. Big deal! I am getting good grades. I do my chores. I help with my baby sister. I sure hope this doctor does not give me a shot. I am going to run right out of there if I see a needle!"

"Come on Zola!" Daddy yelled from the kitchen.

Mommy, Daddy, Zola and her baby sister, Zuri all loaded up into the shiny red Volkswagen. The ride to the Medical College of Virginia Hospital was short and boring. Once they arrived, Zola walked right up to the door with the word AUDIOLOGIST printed on it. Zola tried to pronounce the word, "Au-di-olo-gist."

"Very good Zola," said Mommy.

Zola and her family sat down in the waiting room and waited to be called. Suddenly the door opened. A very pretty lady with dark colored hair and the friendliest eyes she had ever seen appeared before her.

"Hi Zola. My name is Dr. Jacee and I am going to take good care of you. Will you follow me to the back?"

"Mommy?" Zola turned around pleading with her eyes for her mother to come with her.

"You watch the baby. I will go back with Zola," Mommy said to Daddy.

Zola and Mommy followed Dr. Jacee to a small room and inside that small room was another small room with a door. Zola looked around. There were toys and all kinds of wires and buttons outside of the room.

"Okay, Zola, I want you to sit in this booth. I am going to give you this button and put this headset over your ears. When you hear the beep, I want you to push the button. I am going to close the door so that it will be really quiet and you can hear the beeps, but Mommy and I are sitting right outside the box. If you get scared or need us, just speak out loud in the box and we will open the door right away."

Zola sat in the box and listened for the beeps. She listened really hard, but the higher the sound, the more difficult it became for her to hear the beeps.

"Okay, Zola, you have done very well. Now I am going to say some words and I want you to repeat after me," said Dr. Jacee.

Zola repeated the words as best she could, but quickly grew very frustrated. "Did she say baseball or hotdog? Maybe it was ice cream. UGH!"

Zola scowled. "This is a lot harder than it looks."

"Alright Zola," Dr. Jacee said. "Let's get you unhooked and out of here so that we can talk with Mommy and Daddy. You did an excellent job young lady!"

Zola, Mommy and Dr. Jacee all went back to the waiting room to get Zuri and Daddy. Then Dr. Jacee walked them all down to a small conference room.

Dr. Jacee said, "Zola, I am going to make some molds of your ears so that I know what size ears you have."

Next, she took some silly putty and put it into Zola's ears. Zola giggled. The silly putty was cold and tickled as it filled her ear canal. Zola sat for about 10 minutes until the molds became hard and retained their shape.

Then, Dr. Jacee took them out and placed them in a small cardboard box. Wow, Zola thought. I have some very tiny ears, as she looked over into the box.

Mommy, Daddy and Dr. Jacee all began to talk. Zola could not really hear them anyway, so she busied herself by playing with her baby sister, Zuri.

As she tried to eavesdrop, she heard words like, "Overcome the challenges of hearing loss, optimal speech understanding, social interaction, and successful learning." She really did not understand what it all meant until she thought she heard something about "hearing aids."

"Zola come over here and sit with us," said Mommy.

"Zola, the test that you did in the booth shows that you have some hearing loss," Dr. Jacee said. "It is not your fault, but we don't really know what has caused you to lose a portion of your hearing. It is very important for us to get you some hearing aids to help you hear better. Do you know what hearing aids are?"

"Yes," Zola quickly replied. "They are these really UGLY things that old Uncle Brown puts in his ears. They make his ears stick out and look funny. They whistle and make all kinds of noises!"

Zola started to cry. "I don't want hearing aids. Everyone is going to make fun of me at school! Mommy! Daddy! Please don't make me wear hearing aids!" Zola sobbed so hard that her baby sister ran to her to give her a hug.

"Zola, Zola," Dr. Jacee said as she tried to calm Zola down. "We have all different colors and types of hearing aids for you. They will help you hear and be comfortable. I would even suggest you learn sign language."

Oh no, Zola thought, now they want me to have blue or red machines sticking out of my head and talk with my fingers. I will look like a space creature. I have seen people talking with their fingers before at school and that is just so weird. I am going to be teased so badly! I can never go back to my school again! Zola continued to cry. She was angry, frightened and sad, all at the same time.

If only Mrs. Smith had minded her business and left me alone! This is all her fault, Zola thought to herself.

"I apologize for my daughter," Daddy said to Dr. Jacee.

"It is most understandable that your daughter has reacted this way. This is going to be a huge adjustment for her. It will take some getting used to, but she will understand and appreciate it later on in life when she is older."

Daddy picked Zola up in his arms and gave her a big hug. Zola's crying exhausted her. This is my safe place, Zola thought as she drifted off to sleep in her Daddy's strong arms.

A few weeks passed by and one day Mommy got a phone call. The call was to let Zola and her parents know that the hearing aids had come in and were ready for pick up.

Chapter 3

This time it was just Mommy and Zola that went to the doctor. Daddy had to work and Zuri was at the babysitter's house. Dr. Jacee brought in two small light brown hearing aids. She put the molds in her ears and tucked the small plastic tube and hearing aid itself behind Zola's ear. She did something in her computer on the desk and Zola heard a series of beeps and all of a sudden, Zola could hear a light roaring sound.

"Dr. Jacee! Dr. Jacee!" Zola exclaimed. Her eyes were wide with excitement. "What is that sound?"

"You are hearing the sound of the air conditioner blowing," said Dr. Jacee.

Zola closed her eyes. "Dr. Jacee, I think I hear a cat."

"No, Zola. You are hearing a baby crying in the next room over."

Mommy looked at Zola and smiled. She was so happy to see her daughter happy, as Zola had certainly cried enough over the last few weeks.

"Ok, Zola, let's try out your new hearing aids. Into the booth you go young lady. Same as before, beeps and words. Are you ready?"

"Yes," Zola said confidently. She did MUCH better in the booth the second time. She was able to hear the high and low beeps so much better and she even got the words right! Baseball, ice cream, hot dog! Zola jumped up and down in her seat with excitement.

"Very good Zola!" said Dr. Jacee. "Are you ready to look into the mirror and see what your new hearing aids look like now?"

Dr. Jacee stood Zola in front of the mirror. Zola suddenly felt like someone had let all the air out of her body. She stared at the girl in the mirror looking back at her. This girl had these brown tubes coming out of her ears and these very noticeable "things" sitting behind her ears. Zola had totally forgotten about the excitement she felt from being able to hear sounds she had never heard before. Tears started to slowly flow down her face while she stared at the new Zola looking back at her in the mirror.

Mommy quietly moved in behind Zola. She knelt down beside her daughter on the floor. She turned Zola around and looked deep into her daughter's sad brown eyes.

"Zola, Mommy loves you very much. I know that you can't really understand all that is going on with you now, but everyone is created special. You were created special with hearing loss. You are a funny, sweet, and intelligent young lady. These hearing aids do not define who you are inside, but rather help you to become the great person you are going to be one day. I know that you hate it now, but it is all to help you hear, speak and understand others better. Even as a very little girl your life's purpose is already clear, to uplift and inspire others around you that also have challenges. Mommy wants you to always remember that we will treat you no differently from your sister. You are still Zola, the sky's the limit and you can do and become anything you want to do and become. Always remember to reach for the moon and if you don't get there, you will surely grab a star."

Zola reached her arms around Mommy's neck and gave her a big hug and just cried her eyes out in her mother's arms.

The very next day Zola wore her new hearing aids to school. Everyone was very curious about these new "things" Zola had in her ears. The kids in her class surrounded her with their questions.

"Do they hurt?" Frankie asked.

"No," said Zola.

"Are they really loud?" asked Michelle.

"No," Zola said again.

The others stared in amazement as they checked out Zola's ears. All of a sudden, the class bully, Mikey, walked up to Zola.

"Look at the deaf girl," he said as he laughed right in Zola's face.

Zola almost broke down, right then and there, but she remembered what her mommy said to her the day before.

She looked right into Mikey's face and said, "Leave me alone right now!"

Her best friend, Tonya, stood beside her in her defense. "Mikey if you don't leave Zola alone right this instant, we will tell Mrs. Smith on you."

Mikey rolled his eyes and went back to his seat. The kids did not know it, but Mrs. Smith had been standing at the door listening to the children's conversation all along.

"Good morning class," she said as she walked into the room. She walked right over to Zola and placed a note on her desk. The note said, I am very proud of how you stood up for yourself today and you will be just fine. Mrs. Smith took her place at her desk in front of the room and looked over the children in her room. "Listen up children I have something to say." All of the children turned their attention to their teacher.

"I want to make it very clear that I will not tolerate bullying in this classroom. Everyone is born into this world different.

Differences are what make each of you special and unique. Some of you cannot see very well, so you wear glasses. Some of you have a hard time focusing and staying on task, so you take medications. Now we have a student that did not hear very well, but now she can because she has hearing aids. I want you all to understand that having a disability does not define who you are on the inside. A person is defined by what lies within their heart, not what is seen on the outside. In this classroom, we will all treat each other with respect, be friendly, and continue to include one another in our daily classroom team activities. Do I make myself clear?"

"Yes ma'am," the class said all together.

"Very well, now please turn to page 26 in your history books."

Making eye contact with Zola, Mrs. Smith gave her a private wink. Zola responded with a shy smile. Zola pulled out her history book, smiled quietly and thought to herself, Mommy, Daddy and Mrs. Smith were right, everything is going to be just fine.

About the Author

Narita Snead is a loving wife and mother to 3 boys. She is a board certified nurse practitioner and nonprofit founder. She wrote this book to tell all of the boys and girls who are BORN DIFFERENT,

"It is o.k. to dream."

Made in United States
North Haven, CT
16 October 2023

42825003R00027